DISASTERS AND THE ENVIRONMENT

HURRICANES
and the Environment

by Ailynn Collins

CAPSTONE PRESS
a capstone imprint

Published by Capstone Press, an imprint of Capstone
1710 Roe Crest Drive, North Mankato, Minnesota 56003
capstonepub.com

Copyright © 2025 by Capstone. All rights reserved. No part of this publication may be reproduced in whole or in part, or stored in a retrieval system, or transmitted in any form or by any means, electronic, mechanical, photocopying, recording, or otherwise, without written permission of the publisher.

Library of Congress Cataloging-in-Publication Data
Names: Collins, Ailynn, 1964- author.
Title: Hurricanes and the environment / by Ailynn Collins.
Description: North Mankato, Minnesota : Capstone Press, [2025]
Series: Disasters and the environment | Includes bibliographical references and index.
Audience: Ages 8-11 | Audience: Grades 4-6
Summary: "Strong winds, heavy rainfall, and huge waves are alldangers of hurricanes. Their force affects not only people but also the environment. Trees in mangrove forests can die. Animals' homes and nesting areas can be destroyed. Some animals can even be carried miles away from their homes. Learn about the steps people can take to help affected areas recover from these fierce ocean storms"-- Provided by publisher.
Identifiers: LCCN 2023051159 (print) | LCCN 2023051160 (ebook) | ISBN 9781669070917 (hardcover) | ISBN 9781669071075 (paperback) | ISBN 9781669071082 (pdf) | ISBN 9781669071105 (kindle edition) | ISBN 9781669071099 (epub)
Subjects: LCSH: Hurricanes--Juvenile literature. | Hurricanes--Environmental aspects--Juvenile literature.
Classification: LCC QC944.2 .C66 2025 (print) | LCC QC944.2 (ebook) | DDC 551.55/2--dc23/eng/20231117
LC record available at https://lccn.loc.gov/2023051159
LC ebook record available at https://lccn.loc.gov/2023051160

Editorial Credits
Editor: Carrie Sheely; Designer: Bobbie Nuytten; Media Researcher: Jo Miller;
Production Specialist: Whitney Schaefer

Image Credits
Alamy: AB Forces News Collection , 15, Kevin Schafer, 22; AP Photo: The Canadian Press, Mike Dembeck, 5; Getty Images: apomares, 29, Bloomberg, 27, John Coletti, 8, Orlando Sentinel, 23 (top), Warren Faidley, 7; NASA: Image courtesy of Mike Trenchard, 9; Photo by FEMA Federal Emergency Management Agency, 25; Shutterstock: Akarawut, 19, Andrea Izzotti, 13, Dan Oberly, 16, Fotopogledi, 12, FotoRequest, 21, Francisco Blanco, Cover (bottom), 11, GraphicsRF.com, 17, Juergen Faelchle, 18, pp1, 20, rtem, 23 (bottom), Ryan Hohm, 26, SARIN KUNTHONG, Cover (top); SuperStock: Reed, Jim, 6; U.S. Air Force photo by Senior Airman Kristen Pittman, 28

Design Elements
Shutterstock: Altitude Visual, ivn3da

Any additional websites and resources referenced in this book are not maintained, authorized, or sponsored by Capstone. All product and company names are trademarks™ or registered® trademarks of their respective holders.

Printed and bound in the USA. PO 5853

TABLE OF CONTENTS

INTRODUCTION
Carried Away!.................. 4

CHAPTER ONE
Big Ocean Storms............... 6

CHAPTER TWO
Damage to Coastlines.......... 10

CHAPTER THREE
Inland Impacts................ 16

CHAPTER FOUR
What Happens to Animals?..... 20

CHAPTER FIVE
Humans and Hurricanes........ 24

Glossary 30
Read More 31
Internet Sites 31
Index...................... 32
About the Author 32

Words in **bold** are in the glossary.

Introduction

CARRIED AWAY!

In September 2010, Hurricane Earl swept over several countries in the Atlantic Ocean. It destroyed homes, downed trees, and toppled power lines. The hurricane flooded towns and cities. Many animals were injured, and the storm destroyed many animal **habitats**.

One animal that became injured in the storm was a brown pelican. These pelicans can be found along the Atlantic coast from northern Virginia to Peru. But this pelican was picked up by strong winds and carried all the way to Canada. She was lost and alone in a strange place that was much colder than she was used to.

Luckily, she was rescued and sent to a wildlife shelter in Canada. The bird was named Ralph. Ralph was later sent to a wildlife center in North Carolina. In the summer of 2011, Ralph was released back into a forest in North Carolina to live free again.

Ralph sits in the wildlife shelter in Canada awaiting her return to the United States.

Chapter One

BIG OCEAN STORMS

Hurricanes are huge storms that form over the warm waters of the Atlantic Ocean or eastern Pacific Ocean. Around the world, hurricanes may be called cyclones or typhoons. They usually occur between June and November each year. These storms come with powerful winds and large amounts of rain. The winds push the sea toward the land, creating high walls of water that crash into coastlines. This rise in water is called a storm surge. This is the most destructive part of a hurricane.

Storm surges that flood roads can be dangerous for motorists.

Hurricane Irma's storm surge affected coastlines near Miami, Florida, in 2017.

FACT

The tallest storm surge was 42 feet (12.8 meters). It happened in 1899 during Tropical Cyclone Mahina.

Scientists believe that hurricanes are becoming more dangerous. As the oceans grow warmer because of **climate** change, hurricanes will hold more moisture in them. They will move more slowly over the land and be more intense.

7

Hurricanes can cause a lot of destruction. They can cause billions of dollars in damage to cities. Many people can be killed or injured. Fish, birds, and other animals that live in the paths of these storms can be affected too. The **environment** can also experience terrible effects from these storms. Let's take a closer look at how hurricanes affect nature.

A hurricane's strong winds can snap trees.

A Giant Cage

Hurricanes whirl in a giant cone shape. In the middle of this cone is the eye of the storm. It is quiet and still. The eye can act as a giant cage to hold whatever is swept up inside. Shorebirds such as sandpipers can be carried far inland, a long way from their homes.

Chapter Two

DAMAGE TO COASTLINES

Hurricanes start in the ocean. They hit the coastlines and bring heavy rains. They dump so much water that the land floods almost instantly.

Mangrove forests grow near coasts. They provide homes for many types of fish and other sea life. Mangroves live in **brackish** water. This water is half salt water and half fresh water. Hurricane rains bring a lot of fresh water. This disturbs the balance of the brackish water, making it less salty. Hurricanes can also bring salt water from the ocean to the coast. Then the water is too salty for the mangroves. Survival becomes difficult for the trees and the creatures that live there. Without these forests, coastlines would be in danger of disappearing. Mangrove forests protect coastlines from **erosion**.

In 2017, Hurricane Irma damaged large sections of mangrove forests in southern Florida. Scientists found that about 83 percent of the mangrove forests recovered after a year. But part of the forests never recovered. Scientists think they could have been damaged by too much salt water.

One of the mangrove forests damaged by Hurricane Irma was in Florida's Everglades National Park.

Damage to Coral Reefs

Coral reefs also protect coastlines. Without them, beaches get pulled back into the sea and erode completely. Reefs are known as rain forests of the sea. They provide food and shelter to more than 1 million **species** of animals.

Stony corals have skeletons made of limestone. Reefs are made up of these corals.

Hurricane winds stir the seawater. This causes sand to come up to the surface, blocking sunlight. Without sunlight, coral reefs cannot grow. Without reefs, fish, eels, turtles, and more can die.

When coral reefs die, the animals that depend on them often cannot survive.

Restoring Beaches

Beaches lose sand during a hurricane. If left alone, the sea will slowly push sand back onto the beaches. It could take months to years.

People can help restore beaches by bringing in sand from other places. It's important that the new sand comes from a nearby area with similar vegetation and climate.

Engineers once believed that building seawalls and retaining walls at beaches would protect the sand from being lost. However, they soon realized that it was better to work with nature to help beaches recover. They could plant grasses that trapped sand as it blew in the wind. They could also help by cleaning up **contaminated** water and wastewater spills. Time and nature would then help a new shoreline grow back.

Case Study
Hurricane Maria

The El Yunque National Forest in Puerto Rico was hit by Hurricane Maria in 2017. The storm caused major damage to human, plant, and animal life. The island is still trying to recover from the terrible storm.

The hurricane damaged forests there. Winds ripped trees away from their roots. They then were not able to absorb water and **nutrients** from the soil. But many trees can withstand damage. Mangroves and rain forests that were damaged by the flooding are slowly growing back again.

Chapter Three

INLAND IMPACTS

Hurricanes can affect areas far beyond the coast. In 2005, Hurricane Katrina destroyed more than 320 million trees. The large number of trees decaying at the same time added a lot of **carbon dioxide** to the air. Scientists believe too much of this gas in the air is a reason for global warming.

In a hurricane, trees are often uprooted and damaged in large numbers. Winds are so strong they can strip the bark right off the trees. In Hurricane Katrina, the wind speeds were up to 140 miles (225 kilometers) per hour. Many trees looked as if they had been scraped with sandpaper.

When bark is stripped from trees, they are at risk from disease.

Winds also blow away seeds. New trees can't grow in their usual place. New seeds from plants that are not native to the area may be carried in. This can greatly change the face of the forests.

The Natural Cycle of Trees

Trees use energy from the sun to absorb carbon dioxide and make food. This process is called photosynthesis. They use carbon to make food and release oxygen into the air. When trees die, they decay. They release carbon dioxide back into the air. This is part of the natural cycle.

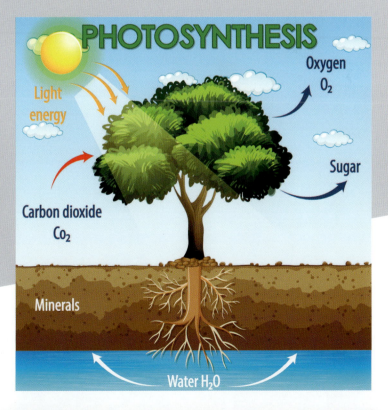

Hurricane rainstorms also flood the land. Tree roots cannot handle that much water in the soil, and they drown. Hurricanes may carry salt from ocean water. The roots are unable to absorb salty water. They die from this as well.

Recovery and Restoration

The most natural way to allow forests to recover is to let them do it on their own. This, however, can take decades or hundreds of years.

Forest scientists can help with **restoration**. In some cases, trees can be pruned in preparation for large storms. People cut off old or damaged branches.

Large areas can be replanted after storm damage.

Pruning makes the trees stronger so that they better withstand storms. Afterward, their recovery may only take two to five years. Trees that are too damaged by storms can be cut away, and their wood can be used for timber.

People can also help with reforesting. They can plant trees that grow back quickly, such as conifers. They may also plant trees that are more tolerant to flooded soil.

People plant mangrove trees.

Chapter Four

WHAT HAPPENS TO ANIMALS?

Hurricanes greatly affect land animals. Many animals lose their homes and their food sources. Small animals can't find food because there's too much debris on forest floors.

Water creatures are also harmed. When salt water mixes with fresh water, fish can die. When beaches are destroyed, sea turtles lose their nests, and crabs lose their homes.

Dolphins and other animals may die when they are carried onto shore by a hurricane.

Another effect of hurricanes is food chain disturbance. Floods can drown rats and other rodents. These are food for birds of prey and other large animals. After Hurricane Sandy in 2012, many hawks and owls near New Jersey had to move to other areas. Their food was in short supply. With predators leaving the area, other smaller birds that didn't live there before moved in.

After Hurricane Sandy, scientists in New Jersey found that they had more finches than ever before.

FACT

Researchers have discovered that sharks can tell if a hurricane is coming up to two weeks ahead of time. These animals can feel a change in the pressure underwater.

Helping Animals Recover

After a hurricane, scientists often go to beaches and forests to check wildlife loss. Volunteers help to count one species at a time.

An example is the Puerto Rican parrot. There aren't many of these parrots left in the world. Before Hurricane Maria, scientists had counted about 600 birds in the El Yunque National Forest. After the hurricane, they could find only 470.

Puerto Rican parrot

After a hurricane, it's important to begin the repair and rebuilding of national parks and wildlife refuges. Animal welfare groups work on rescuing and relocating animals that have been displaced. Scientists work to restore animal habitats. These include coastal marshes, wetlands, shorelines, and forests. Overall, recovery from a hurricane can take years for some animal species. But in time, many do come back.

After Hurricane Maria, people restored sand dunes on beaches.

Case Study
Hurricane Andrew

In 1992, Hurricane Andrew killed more than 9 million fish in the seas near Louisiana by pushing them out of the water and onto land. In the areas around Florida, scientists believe 182 million fish were killed by this storm. The violence of the ocean water was to blame for much of it. Inland, the added salt water to the fresh water killed fish that were unable to live with high levels of salt.

Chapter Five

HUMANS AND HURRICANES

Hurricanes have a big impact on people as well. It is believed that hurricanes cause the deaths of about 10,000 people each year. Homes and businesses are destroyed. Ordinary items can become dangerous flying missiles in the strong winds. People are cut off from resources such as clean water and shelter.

Hurricane Idalia hit Florida, Georgia, and South Carolina at the end of August 2023. Many towns were flooded. Homes were swept away by water, and more than 300,000 people lost power. People in Florida reported having to swim out through their windows to get to safety.

In the United States, government agencies such as the Federal Emergency Management Agency (FEMA) often help with recovery. They rescue stranded people. They provide temporary shelter, water, food, and clothing. After Hurricane Andrew, FEMA set up a tent city for those who lost their homes.

FEMA workers in Atlanta, Georgia, begin response operations for Hurricane Idalia.

25

Cleaning Up

After a hurricane, people need to clean up debris from damaged homes and buildings. Special companies clean up poisons and pollution from broken sewer pipes, landfills, and chemical plants.

A worker in a bulldozer cleans up a beach in Mexico.

Case Study
Cyclone Idai

Hurricanes are called cyclones when they form over the South Pacific and Indian Oceans. In March 2019, Cyclone Idai hit the nations of Mozambique, Malawi, and Zimbabwe on the southeast coast of Africa. It's believed that 1,000 people died. Thousands more were injured by the storm. Most of the houses in the city of Beira, Mozambique, were damaged or destroyed. As a result of the flooding, people became sick with waterborne diseases. Landslides cut towns off from the bigger cities. As a result, some victims couldn't get help or clean drinking water for a while. Many people had little to no food. Six weeks later, Cyclone Kenneth also hit Mozambique. It made the situation there even worse.

We can't avoid hurricanes, but we can prepare to face them. Scientists continue to study hurricanes. Computer models can predict how much storm surge a hurricane will bring. Some scientists travel in airplanes through a hurricane's eye to study a storm. This helps people make better predictions about a storm's strength.

FACT
Members of the U.S. Air Force and the National Oceanic and Atmospheric Administration fly into hurricanes. They are called Hurricane Hunters.

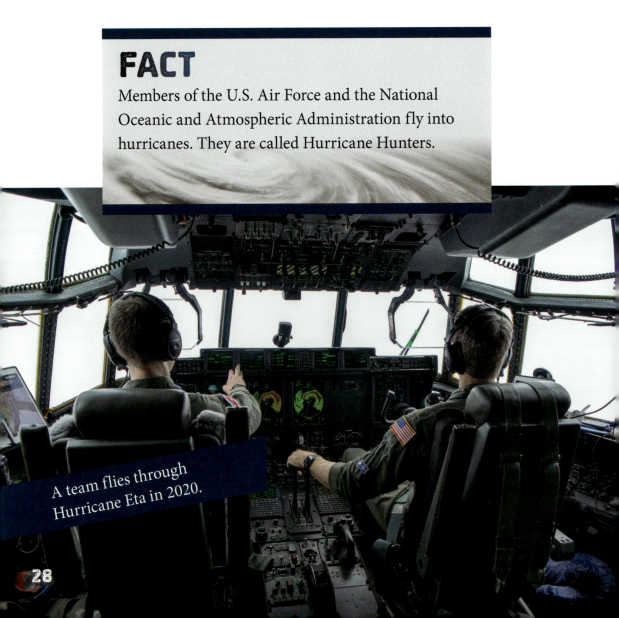

A team flies through Hurricane Eta in 2020.

After a hurricane, the long process of recovery begins. How can people help? People can offer to help clean beaches. They can help organizations replant trees. They can support groups that are involved in habitat recovery and animal rescue. Humans, animals, and the environment are all dependent on one another. By working together, we may be able to shorten recovery times after these strong storms.

Debris cleanup can help beaches recover.

Glossary

carbon dioxide (KAHR-buhn dy-AHK-syd)—a gas in the air that animals give off and plants use to make food

climate (KLY-muht)—the usual weather that occurs in a place

contaminate (kuhn-TA-muh-nayt)—to make dirty or unfit for use

environment (in-VY-ruhn-muhnt)—the natural world of the land, water, and air

erosion (i-ROH-zhuhn)—wearing away of rock or soil by wind, water, or ice

habitat (HAB-uh-tat)—the natural place and conditions in which a plant or animal lives

nutrient (NOO-tree-ent)—a substance needed by a living thing to stay healthy

restoration (re-stuh-RAY-shuhn)—the act of bringing something back to its former condition

species (SPEE-sheez)—a group of plants or animals that share common characteristics

Read More

Crane, Cody. *All About Hurricanes: Discovering Earth's Wildest Storms.* New York: Children's Press, 2022.

Klatte, Kathleen A. *Hurricanes.* Buffalo, NY: Rosen Publishing, 2023.

Suen, Anastasia. *Hurricanes.* Mankato, MN: Amicus Ink, 2021.

Internet Sites

Kids.Earth.org: 6 Amazing Facts About Mangrove Trees for Kids
kids.earth.org/life-in-the-water/facts-about-mangrove-trees/

National Geographic Kids: Hurricanes
kids.nationalgeographic.com/science/article/hurricane

Weather WizKids: Hurricanes
weatherwizkids.com/weather-hurricane.htm

Index

animals, 4, 5, 8, 12, 13, 20, 21, 22, 29

beaches, 12, 14, 20, 22, 23, 26, 29

climate change, 7
coral reefs, 12, 13
Cyclone Idai, 27

erosion, 10, 12
eyes, 9, 28

Federal Emergency Management Agency (FEMA), 25
flooding, 4, 6, 10, 15, 18, 19, 21, 24, 27

Hurricane Andrew, 23, 25
Hurricane Earl, 4
Hurricane Idalia, 24, 25
Hurricane Irma, 7, 11
Hurricane Katrina, 16
Hurricane Maria, 15, 22, 23
Hurricane Sandy, 21

mangrove forests, 10, 11, 15

reforestation, 19
restoration, 18

salt water, 10, 11, 18, 20, 23
storm surges, 6, 7, 28

trees, 4, 8, 10, 15, 16, 17, 18, 19, 29

About the Author

Ailynn Collins has written many books for children. They include stories about aliens and monsters to books about science, space, and the future. These are her favorite subjects. She lives outside Seattle with her family and six dogs. When she's not writing, she enjoys participating in dog shows and dog sports.